D1506018

THE BRIDE'S BOUQUET

About the Author

Jeanne Graham gained an appreciation for flowers as a young child, helping tend her Grandmother's flower garden on family visits. As an adult she went on to open her own successful floral design business, Blue Sage Inc., focusing on event decorating. She has designed and produced the florals for hundreds of beautiful weddings since tying her first bouquet in 1991.

Convinced of the need for a more specialized book that floral designers could use during consultations, she began work on *The Bride's Bouquet*. She resides in Baltimore with her husband Geoff Graham and daughter Delaney.

Acknowledgments

This book would never have come to fruition without the dedicated and talented work of our staff and the support of my friends and family. Carla Anderson, Ken Goodman, Stacy Korzelius, and Barbe Sawicki designed and crafted many of the bouquets in this book. Models Jen Johnson, Sandra Taylor and Catherine Trost patiently posed late into the evenings.

Other friends, associates, and vendors are obliged thanks for lending assistance at key moments. Miles Anderson, Robin Newman, Mike Northrup, Rob Randolph, and Sarah Trost helped with many of the technical details associated with producing this book. Amarosa Farms, Delaware Valley, Schaeffer's, Van Delft, and Wilmington Wholesale Florists went out of their way to provide us with superb florals. Gala Cloths and Select Event Rentals supplied us with an abundance of linens and chairs for our sets. All the beautiful gowns you see in this book were provided by Gamberdella's, whom I can't thank enough for their generosity.

Jeanne Graham

Index

1 2 3 4 5 6 7 8 9

10 11 12 13 14 15 16 17 18

19 20 21 22 23 24 25 26 27

28 29 30 31 32 33 34 35 36

37 38 39 40 41 42 43 44 45

46 47 48 49 50 51 52 53 54

55 56 57 58 59 60 61 62 63

64 65 66 67 68 69 70 71 72

1

GREEN HYDRANGEA • GOLDEN SOLIDAGO • SOFT YELLOW FREESIA • PEARLED STEPHANOTIS
BLUE DELPHINIUM • ESKIMO ROSES • VERSILIA ROSES

French Tulips • Variegated Lily Grass

3

4

HOT PRINCESS ROSES • FEMMA ROSES • KONFETTI ROSES
PALE YELLOW FREESIA • VARIEGATED PITTOSPORUM

5

WHITE HYDRANGEA • HEATHER • BRUNIA ALBIFLORA • BLUE AGAPANTHUS
PINE • CEDAR • WHITE BIRCH

HYDRANGEA

YELLOW ALSTROEMERIA • PLUM CALLA LILIES • VARIEGATED TULIPS • YELLOW KING ROSES

HOCUS POCUS ROSES • SKYLINE ROSES

9

VENDELLA ROSES • CREAM STOCK • WHITE STOCK • VARIEGATED PITTOSPORUM

Vogue Roses • Titanic Roses • Vendella Roses
Blush Pink Spray Roses • Pitosforum Nigra

11

JUDY ROSES • GOLDEN SOLIDAGO • YELLOW FREESIA • VARIEGATED PITTOSPORUM

12

WHITE RANUNCULUS • PALE YELLOW TULIPS • CREAM LISIANTHUS • LEMON LEAF
MINIATURE CREAM GERBERA DAISIES • WHITE LILACS • WHITE SWEET PEAS

13

14

RED INTUITION ROSES • PALE PINK NERINE LILIES • GREEN ICE HONEYCOMB GINGER

15

PURPLE VERONICA • PINK CURCUMA • YELLOW AND WHITE IRIS
BEAR GRASS • EUCALYPTUS PARVIFOLIA • RAFFIA

16

Longiflorum Lilies • Femma Roses

GRACIAS SPRAY ROSES • MACARENA SPRAY ROSES

19

PURPLE HYACINTH • BRUNIA ALBIFLORA • BOXWOOD

21
WHITE CALLA LILIES • VARIEGATED PITTOSPORUM

22

CREAM FRENCH TULIPS • MESSAGE ROSES • PINK NERINE LILIES • MAGENTA FREESIA
PINK STOCK • MERRY WIDOW TULIPS • MINIATURE VARIEGATED MYRTLE

23

BLUE DELPHINIUM • BLUE THISTLE • MACARENA SPRAY ROSES
KONFETTI ROSES • ORANGE KANGAROO PAWS • BOXWOOD

BIRDS OF PARADISE • TEPE FOLIAGE

MESSAGE ROSES • PAPAYA ROSES • AALSMEER GOLD ROSES

26

BLACK MAGIC ROSES • MANGO CALLA LILIES • BRONZE FREESIA • CALCYNIA
GOLDEN SOLIDAGO • HONEY FLAIR HYPERICUM BERRIES • LEMON LEAF

PURPLE LISIANTHUS • BLUE STREAM LIMONIUM • VIBURNUM • EUCALYPTUS PARVIFOLIA

28

29

LIMON ROSES • MIRACLE ROSES • ORANGE RANUNCULUS • VIBURNUM
GOLDEN YELLOW ORNITHOGALUM • TREASURE CALLA LILIES

Miniature Gerbera Daisies • Blue Eucalyptus

31

BUPLEURUM • WHEAT • JADE HYPERICUM BERRIES • KERMIT BUTTON MUMS

32

AKITO ROSES • WHITE FREESIA • WHITE STOCK • CREAM TULIPS
WHITE SWEETPEAS • PITOSFORUM NIGRA

33

MAGENTA BRAIN CELOSIA • VARIEGATED LILY GRASS • SALVIA

34

BLACK MAGIC ROSES • PURPLE SWEET PEAS • ORANGE TULIPS
RED TULIPS • YELLOW FREESIA • LEMON LEAF

35

CANDY BIANCA ROSES • PALE PINK HYACINTH • HOT PINK LYSIMACHIA • GYPSOPHILA

36

MAGENTA BRAIN CELOSIA

38

SONIA ROSES • BLACK MAGIC ROSES • AUBERGINE CALLA LILIES
PEACH SPRAY ROSES • PITOSFORUM NIGRA

39

PEONIES • STOCK • VIRGINIA ROSES • PEARLED STEPHANOTIS • BEAR GRASS • SEA SHELLS

Gardenias • Pearled Purple Hyacinth Florets • Light Blue Hydrangea

41

GREEN CYMBIDIUM ORCHIDS • BEAR GRASS

43

BURGUNDY PEONIES • HYPERICUM BERRIES • BLACK BACARRA ROSES
MACARENA SPRAY ROSES • FRESH WHEAT • LEUCODENDRON

HELLEBORUS • BLACK BEAUTY ROSES • ESKIMO ROSES

45

PALE PINK LISIANTHUS • DOUBLE YELLOW TULIPS • BLACK WIDOW KANGAROO PAWS • CEDAR

MINITURE GERBERA DAISIES • ORANGE UNIQUE ROSES • CONGA ROSES • IVY

47

BLACK MAGIC ROSES • BLACK BEAUTY ROSES • RED SPRAY ROSES • ORANGE MOKARA ORCHIDS
ESKIMO ROSES • SPICY ROSES • PURPLE ANEMONES • HYPERICUM BERRIES

Mokara Orchids • Magenta Freesia • Circus Roses • Black Magic Roses • Leucodendron

49

AUBERGINE CALLA LILIES • LIATRIS • PURPLE LILACS • SILVER KING ARTMESIA • BEAR GRASS

50

WHITE PEONIES • LILAC FREESIA • BLUE CURIOSA ROSES • LAVENDER STOCK
MANGO CALLA LILIES • LIMONIUM • CREAM STOCK • AKITO ROSES

51

CHARTREUSE DENDROBIUM ORCHIDS • GREEN GODDESS CALLA LILIES • LUCKY BAMBOO • BEAR GRASS

52

YEARNING DESERT • PREMATURE SCABIOSA • BRUNIA ALBIFLORA
BLACK DOT ORNITHOGALUM • EUCALYPTUS PARVIFOLIA

PEARLED STEPHANOTIS • PEARLED HYACINTH FLORETS

54

55

FEMMA ROSES • RED FREESIA

57

BLACK MAGIC ROSES • NERINE LILIES • HYPERICUM BERRIES • VARIEGATED PITTOSPORUM

NERINE LILIES

GERBERA DAISIES • HYPERICUM BERRIES • BEAR GRASS

CANDID PROPHYTA ROSES • FRISCO ROSES • MOKARA ORCHIDS
YELLOW CRASPEDIA • SEEDED EUCALYPTUS

61

AUBERGENE CALLA LILIES • HONEY FLAIR HYPERICUM BERRIES • CREAM STOCK
JAMES STOREI ORCHIDS • BLACK BACARRA ROSES • LEMON LEAF

Red Calla Lilies • Black Magic Roses • Hypericum Berries

Pink Mink Protea • Vanity Roses • Tepe Foliage

TITANIC ROSES • PALE PINK ASTILBE • EUCALYPTUS PARVIFOLIA

DUTCH TULIPS

66

White Calla Lilies • Lucky Bamboo

RED TULIPS • RHINESTONE ACCENTS

68
AKITO ROSES • KIKO ROSES • BLACK MAGIC ROSES • WHITE PEONIES
PALE PINK PEONIES • LILAC SWEET PEAS • BLUEBIRD ROSES

69

BLACK MAGIC ROSES

70

GLORIOSA LILIES • BLACK MAGIC ROSES • JUDY ROSES

71

YELLOW SNAPDRAGONS • WHITE SNAPDRAGONS • ACACIA

YELLOW ASIATIC LILIES • VARIEGATED LILY GRASS

BLACK MAGIC ROSES

ORANGE MOKARA ORCHIDS • BLACK MAGIC ROSES • ACACIA • CHINA BERRY

75
WHITE RANUNCULUS • WHITE LILAC • MINIATURE CALLA LILIES
WHITE STOCK • LIGHT BLUE HYDRANGEA

76

MINIATURE CYMBIDIUM ORCHIDS • MINIATURE DAFFODILS • VIBURNUM • GRAPE HYACINTH

77

MAGENTA LYSIMACHIA • WHITE CALLA LILIES • HOT PRINCESS ROSES
PURPLE HYDRANGEA • CYMBIDIUM ORCHIDS • NAGI GREENS

PINK SCABIOSA • PURPLE SALVIA • RED CELOSIA

WHEAT

80

CATTALEYA ORCHIDS • BEAR GRASS

82
YELLOW DAFFODILS • RED FREESIA • PURPLE PHLOX • ORANGE RANUNCULUS

Coral Peony • Antique Velvet Leaves

PINK PEONIES • WHITE FREESIA • MAGENTA STOCK • WAXFLOWER • VOGUE ROSES

DICK WILDEN DAFFODILS

DAFFODILS • WHITE LYSIMACHIA • VIBURNUM • KAMILLE

87
Lilac Sweet Peas • Purple Lisianthus • Grape Hyacinth • Eskimo Roses

88

GIANT PURPLE ALLIUM • PURPLE ANEMONES • LAMBS EAR
SILVER BRUNIA BERRIES • HOSTA LEAVES

89

BURGUNDY RANUNCULUS • ORANGE RANUNCULUS • YELLOW DOUBLE TULIPS • PURPLE LISIANTHUS

90

91

Blue Curiosa Roses • Osiana Roses • Lilac Sweet Peas • Pink Peonies

93

94

BLACK BEAUTY ROSES • WHITE FREESIA • BOXWOOD

GREEN CYMBIDIUM ORCHIDS • BEAR GRASS

96

97

WHITE LISIANTHUS • PINK PEONIES • LAVENDER FREESIA • WHITE STOCK
SOFT PINK SWEET PEAS • PITOSFORUM NIGRA

98

AGERATUM • LEMON LEAF

99

LOVELY LYDIA SPRAY ROSES• LEMON LEAF

100

101

CRASPEDIA • PURPLE VERONICA

Purple Anemones • Purple Lisianthus • White Freesia • Blue Agapanthus • Cedar

103

REBECCA ALSTROEMERIA

104
BANKSIA • GREEN HELLEBORUS • BERZILLIA BERRIES

105

Blue Hydrangea • Green Hydrangea • Hanging Green Amaranthus

107
LYDIA SPRAY ROSES • MAGENTA STOCK • BLACK MAGIC ROSES • PINK CALCYNIA
PINK TULIPS • RED FREESIA • ANTIQUE HYDRANGEA

108

BLACK MAGIC ROSES • MAMBO SPRAY ROSES • AKITO ROSES • WHITE CALCYNIA
HONEY FLAIR HYPERICUM BERRIES • ANTIQUE HYDRANGEA • bronze FREESIA • LEMON LEAF

109

ESKIMO ROSES • BLUE CURIOSA ROSES • STRANGER ROSES • LAVENDER ASTRANTIA • SWORD FERN

LAVENDER STOCK • BRASSICA • BOXWOOD

111

BLACK BEARD WHEAT • RYE • MILLET

CRASPEDIA • BRUNIA ALBIFLORA • LEMON LEAF

WHITE PEONIES • YELLOW ALSTROEMERIA • BLUE DELPHINIUM • SILVER KING ARTMESIA

115

LIGHT BLUE HYDRANGEA • WHITE CYMBIDIUM ORCHIDS • AQUA ROSES • LILAC FREESIA
MAGENTA STOCK • PURPLE SWEET PEAS • ESKIMO ROSES

AQUA ROSES • CURCUMA • BEAR GRASS

117
BURGUNDY PEONIES • ORANGE ASIATIC LILIES • LEUCODENDRON • IVY • JAMES STOREI ORCHIDS

118

MANGO CALLA LILIES • BLACK MAGIC ROSES • HYPERICUM BERRIES
PINK CALCYNIA • VARIEGATED PITTOSPORUM

119
TITANIC ROSES • WHITE PEONIES • WHITE FREESIA • WHITE STOCK • BRASSICA • PINK HEATHER

120

CYMBIDIUM ORCHIDS • DENDROBIUM ORCHIDS • ESKIMO ROSES • LEMON LEAF

121

122

123

RED RANUNCULUS • ORANGE RANUNCULUS • RED BOUVARDIA • SIMPLY RED ROSES
MARLYSE ROSES • VARIEGATED PITTOSPORUM

124
BLACK MAGIC ROSES • SPICY ROSES • KONFETTI ROSES
GREEN HYDRANGEA • MAGENTA STOCK • LILAC FREESIA

125

ESKIMO ROSES • WHITE FREESIA • PEARLED STEPHANOTIS • BLUE DELPHINIUM

126
BLUE HYACINTH • VARIEGATED PITTOSPORUM
RHINESTONE ACCENTS

Pink Peony • Macarena Spray Roses • Blue Curiosa Roses • Heather

128
BLUEBIRD ROSES • HYPERICUM BERRIES • LEUCODENDRON

129

130

KATARINA ROSES • INDIAN FEMMA ROSES • ROSSINI ROSES • PINK SWEET PEAS
PEACH STOCK • VARIEGATED PITOSFORUM NIGRA

131
Red Astilbe • Limonium • Rosemary • Bark Wire Finish

132

WHITE CYMBIDIUM ORCHIDS • WHITE DENDROBIUM ORCHIDS • LILAC FREESIA
PURPLE SWEET PEAS • VANILLA ROSES • LEMON LEAF

133
BLACK MAGIC ROSES • PURPLE TULIPS • MAGENTA STOCK • MIKADO SPRAY ROSES

134

BLACK MAGIC ROSES • ORANGE UNIQUE ROSES • RAVEL ROSES
MINIATURE GERBERA DAISIES • MAGENTA STOCK • VARIEGATED PITOSFORUM NIGRA

135

136

PURPLE LILAC • RICE FLOWER • CHARMES ALSTROEMERIA • WHITE PEONIES • WHITE LILAC

137
CALLA LILIES • DENDROBIUM ORCHIDS • WHITE FREESIA
AKITO ROSES • BLUSH PEONIES • WHITE HYDRANGEA • VARIEGATED PITOSFORUM NIGRA

139

BLUE HYDRANGEA • SUNFLOWERS • BLUE DELPHINIUM • AGERATUM
AKITO ROSES • SKYLINE ROSES • PALE YELLOW FREESIA • LEMON LEAF

140

ESKIMO ROSES • WHITE TULIPS • BLUE SCILLA • LIGHT BLUE HYBRID DELPHINIUM
WHITE FREESIA • VARIEGATED PITOSFORUM NIGRA

PURPLE ANEMONES • LILACS • PURPLE TULIPS • BLACK IRIS • HYDRANGEA

WHITE PEONIES • BLUSH PEONIES • WHITE FREESIA • LILAC SWEET PEAS
AKITO ROSES • OSIANA ROSES

143

AQUA ROSES • LIMONIUM • PITOSFORUM NIGRA

144

145

SAHARA ROSES • HOT CHOCOLATE ROSES • LEMON LEAF

BRONZE FREESIA • BLACK FAN CORAL

147

ESKIMO ROSES • WHITE STOCK • CREAM HYDRANGEA • WHITE FREESIA
LEMON LEAF • RHINESTONE ACCENTS

148

PEARLED STEPHANOTIS

149

BURGUNDY DAHLIAS • GREEN HYDRANGEA • RED HANGING AMARANTHUS

150

151

MANGO CALLA LILIES • LILY GRASS

152

PEONIES

Acacia 71, 74, 105
Agapanthus 5, 102
Ageratum 98, 139, 144
Allium 88, 135
Alstroemeria 7, 103, 114, 122, 135, 136
Amaranthus 106, 149
Amaryllis 80, 152
Anemones 13, 47, 88, 101, 141
Artmesia 19, 49, 114
Astilbe 64, 131
Astrantia 109

Bark Wire 122, 131
Bells of Ireland 13
Berzillia Berries 104
Birds of Paradise 24
Black Beard Wheat 112
Black Fan Coral 146
Bouvardia 123
Brassica 110, 119
Brunia Albiflora 5, 20, 52, 96, 113, 122
Brunia Berries 88
Bupleurum 31

Calcyniass 26, 108, 118
Carnations 129
Celosia 33, 37, 41, 78
China Berry 74
Craspedia 60, 101, 113
Curcuma 15, 116
Curly Willow 100, 144

Daffodils 76, 82, 85, 86
Dahlias 149
Delphinium 1, 23, 54, 114, 125, 139, 140

Eucalyptus 15, 27, 30, 36, 52, 60, 64

Freesia 1, 3, 4, 11, 22, 26, 32, 34, 41, 48,
50, 56, 82, 84, 90, 94, 97, 102, 107, 108,
111, 115, 119, 121, 124, 125, 132, 137,
139, 140, 142, 144, 146, 147

Gardenias 40
Genista 13
Gentiana 19
Gerbera Daisies 3, 12, 30, 46, 59, 134
Grape Hyacinth 76, 87, 90
Gypsophila 35

Heather 4, 119, 122, 127
Helleborus 44, 104
Honeycomb Ginger 14
Hyacinth 20, 35, 40, 53, 126
Hydrangea 1, 4, 6, 40, 75, 77,
105, 106, 107, 108, 115, 124,
137, 139, 141, 147, 149, 150
Hypericum Berries 26, 31, 43, 47,
57, 59, 61, 62, 108, 118, 128

Iris 15, 141

Kamille 86
Kangaroo Paw 23, 45

Leucodendron 43, 48, 117, 128
Liatris 49
Lilac 12, 49, 75, 111, 136, 141, 142
Limonium 27, 50, 131, 143
Lisianthus 12, 27, 28, 45, 87, 89, 97, 102
Lily
  Asiatic 72, 117
  Calla 7, 21, 26, 29, 38, 41, 49, 50, 51,
61, 62, 66, 75, 77, 105, 118, 137, 151
  Gloriosa 70
  Longflorium 17
  Nerine 14, 22, 57, 58
  Lucky Bamboo 51, 66

Lysimachia 19, 35, 77, 86
Millet 112
Mums 3, 31, 105, 150

Orchids
  Cattaleya 81
  Cymbidium 16, 42, 76, 77, 95, 96,
100, 115, 120, 132
  Dendrobium 51, 120, 132, 137
  James Storei 55, 61, 117
  Oncidium 36
  Mokara 47, 48, 60, 74
  Ornithogalum 29, 52

Peonies 39, 43, 50, 68, 83,
84, 91, 92, 93, 97, 111, 114, 117,
119, 127, 136, 137, 138, 142, 153
Pheasant Feathers 55
Phlox 82
Protea
  Pink Mink 63
  Banksia 104, 122
  Pin Cusion 100

Queen Annes Lace 28

Raffia 15
Ranunculus 12, 29, 75,
82, 89, 90, 123
Rhinestone Accents 67, 126, 147
Rice Flower 136
Rosemary 131
Roses
  Aalsmeer Gold 25, 105
  Akito 3, 32, 50, 68, 108, 137, 139, 142
  Aqua 115, 116, 143
  Black Bacarra 43, 61
  Black Beauty 44, 47, 94
  Black Magic 3, 26, 34, 38, 47, 48,
57, 62, 68, 69, 70, 73, 74,
107, 108, 118, 124, 133, 134
  Blue Curiosa 50, 92, 109, 127
  Bluebird 62, 128
  Candid Prophyta 60
  Candy Bianca 35, 121
  Circus 48
  Conga 46
  Eskimo 1, 44, 47, 80, 87,
109, 111, 115, 120, 125, 140, 147
  Femma 4, 17, 56
  Frisco 60
  Hocus Pocus 8, 150
  Hot Chocolate 145
  Hot Princess 4, 77
  Indian Femma 130
  Judy 11, 70
  Katarina 130
  Kiko 68
  Konfetti 4, 23, 124
  Limon 29
  Marlyse 123
  Message 19, 22, 25
  Miracle 29
  Orange Unique 46, 134
  Osiana 92, 142
  Papaya 25
  Ravel 134
  Red Intuition 14
  Rossini 130
  Sahara 145
  Simply Red 123
  Skyline 8, 139
  Sonia 38
  Spicy 47, 124
  Spray 3, 10, 18, 23,
38, 41, 43, 47, 99, 107, 108, 127, 133
  Star 2000 90
  Stranger 109
  Timeless 96

Titanic 10, 64, 119
Vanilla 132
Vanity 63
Vendella 9, 10
Versilia 1, 121
Virginia 39
Vogue 10, 84
Yellow King 7
Rye 112

Salvia 33, 78
Scabiosa 28, 52, 78
Scilla 140
Sea Shells 39
Snapdragons 71
Snow on the Mountain 80
Solidago 1, 11, 26
Statice Sinuata 135
Stephanotis 1, 39, 53, 125, 148
Stock 9, 22, 32, 39, 50,
61, 75, 84, 97, 107, 110, 111,
115, 119, 124, 130, 133, 134, 147
Sunflowers 139
Sweet Peas 12, 32, 34, 68, 87,
92, 97, 115, 130, 132

Thistle 19, 23, 135
Tulips 2, 7, 12, 22, 32, 34,
45, 65, 67, 89, 107, 133, 140, 141, 152

Veronica 15, 101
Viburnum 27, 28, 29, 76, 86

Waxflower 84
Wheat 31, 43, 79
White Birch 5

Yearning Desert 52

Greens

Antique Velvet Leaves 83
Bear Grass 15, 39, 41, 42,
49, 51, 54, 59, 81, 95, 116
Boxwood 16, 20, 23, 94, 96, 110, 129
Cedar 45, 102
Dracena Marginata 121
Hosta Leaves 88, 100
Ivy 46, 117
Kangaroo Grass 55
Lambs Ear 88
Lemon Leaf 12, 26, 34, 61, 98,
99, 108, 111, 113, 120,
132, 139, 145, 147, 152
Lily Grass 54, 151
Miniature Variegated Myrtle 22
Nagi 77
Pine 5
Pitosforum Nigra 10, 32, 38, 97
Snow On The Mountain 80
Sword Fern 109
Tepe Foliage 24, 63
Variegated Lily Grass 2, 33, 72
Variegated Pittosporum 4, 9, 11, 21, 57,
91, 118, 123, 126, 130, 134, 137, 140, 143

Jeanne Graham
Blue Sage Inc.
2118 Cambridge St.
Baltimore, MD 21231

410-675-7090
www.bluesagefloral.com

ISBN 0-9729533-0-2

3524 4531
02/07
Printed in Singapore

Phinium
PUBLICATIONS